Dear parents,

There is nothing more important than teaching our children that God loves us and is always ready to hear our prayers. In fact, God wants us to pray so much that he even gave us a special prayer to say.

For young children, the most natural times to pray are at bedtime and mealtime. Bedtime is a perfect time for prayer, asking God to protect us as we sleep and thanking God for the blessings of the day. Likewise, it is easy to instill in children an attitude of thanks at mealtimes. You might want to set aside time after meals or just before bed to introduce your child to the special prayer that Jesus gave his followers.

It is not difficult for children to learn the words of the Lord's Prayer, but it may take a little more time for them to understand what those words mean. This book is written on a level that a young child will understand, and it includes songs, illustrations, and activities to help each child see how the words of the Lord's Prayer are a part of his or her life, too.

Take the time to read and reread this book with your child. Talk about how each section of the prayer relates to your family and, especially, to your child. You will be amazed at the depth of understanding and faith your child can share with you!

Blessings!

Debbie Trafton O'Neal

Jesus taught his friends many things.
He taught them that God loved them
and cared about what happened to them every day.

I Can Pray with Jesus

The Lord's Prayer for Children

Written by
Debbie Trafton O'Neal

Illustrated by
Taia Morley

Augsburg
MINNEAPOLIS

May you know God's love more and more
as you learn the words of the prayer Jesus taught!

I CAN PRAY WITH JESUS
The Lord's Prayer for Children

Copyright © 1997 Augsburg Fortress
Illustrations copyright © 1997 Taia Morley

The Lord's Prayer on pages 6-25 is from *Praying Together* copyright © 1988 English Language Liturgical Consultation.
Signs on pages 26-27 are based on American Sign Language.
"When I Pray," page 28, copyright © 1959 Sunday School Board, Southern Baptist Convention. Used by permission.

Biblical references for the Lord's Prayer: Matthew 6:9-13, Luke 11:2-4

Cover and book design by Elizabeth Boyce

ISBN 0-8066-3328-X   LCCN 00-00000

The paper used in this publication meets the minimum requirements of American National Standard for Information Sciences—Permanence of Paper for Printed Library Materials, ANSI Z329.48-1984. ∞

AF 9-3328

01   00   4   5   6   7   8   9   10

Jesus often talked with God.
One day Jesus' friends asked him to teach them
how to talk with God, too.

The prayer Jesus taught his friends is called
the Lord's Prayer.

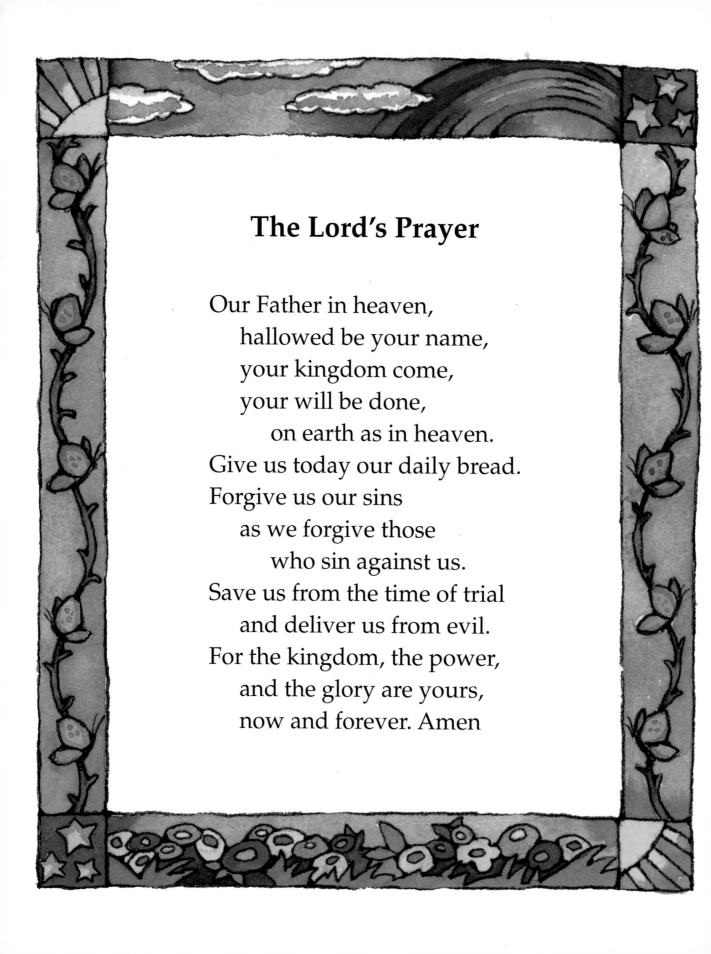

The Lord's Prayer

Our Father in heaven,
   hallowed be your name,
   your kingdom come,
   your will be done,
      on earth as in heaven.
Give us today our daily bread.
Forgive us our sins
   as we forgive those
      who sin against us.
Save us from the time of trial
   and deliver us from evil.
For the kingdom, the power,
   and the glory are yours,
   now and forever. Amen

Jesus Taught His Friends to Pray

 Jesus taught his friends to pray

 a prayer that I know, too.

 A prayer that I can always say
no matter what I do.

 I close my eyes,

 I bow my head,

 I fold my hands to pray.

 Now I'm ready to talk to God
every night and day!

Our Father in heaven,

Dear God,
No matter where I am or what I am doing,
I know you always hear my prayer.

hallowed be your name,

Your name is special, God.
Whenever I hear it,
I remember how wonderful you are
and how much you love me.

your kingdom come,

You have made a beautiful world, God.
I love to wake up to see each new day.
But sometimes I feel grumpy or sad,
and I forget how much you love me.
Then the world doesn't seem so beautiful.
I know you want me to be happy.
So please help me remember that you love me.

your will be done,
on earth as in heaven.

If we lived the way you want us to,
the world would be a better place.
People would care for each other,
and help take care of the world
and everything in it.
Then the world would be a wonderful place,
like you want it to be, God.

Give us today our daily bread.

You give me everything that I need, God.
Good food, and clothes to wear, and a place to sleep.
Thank you for taking care of me.

Forgive us our sins as we forgive those who sin against us.

Sometimes I do things I shouldn't do, God.
Then I'm sorry and I promise not to do it again.
Because you love me very much, you forgive me.

Sometimes other people do things
that make me mad.
I know you can help me
to keep loving people all the time, God.

Save us from the time of trial

God, sometimes I am tempted to do
something I shouldn't do.
Help me to know the difference
between right and wrong.
And help me always to choose what is right.

and deliver us from evil.

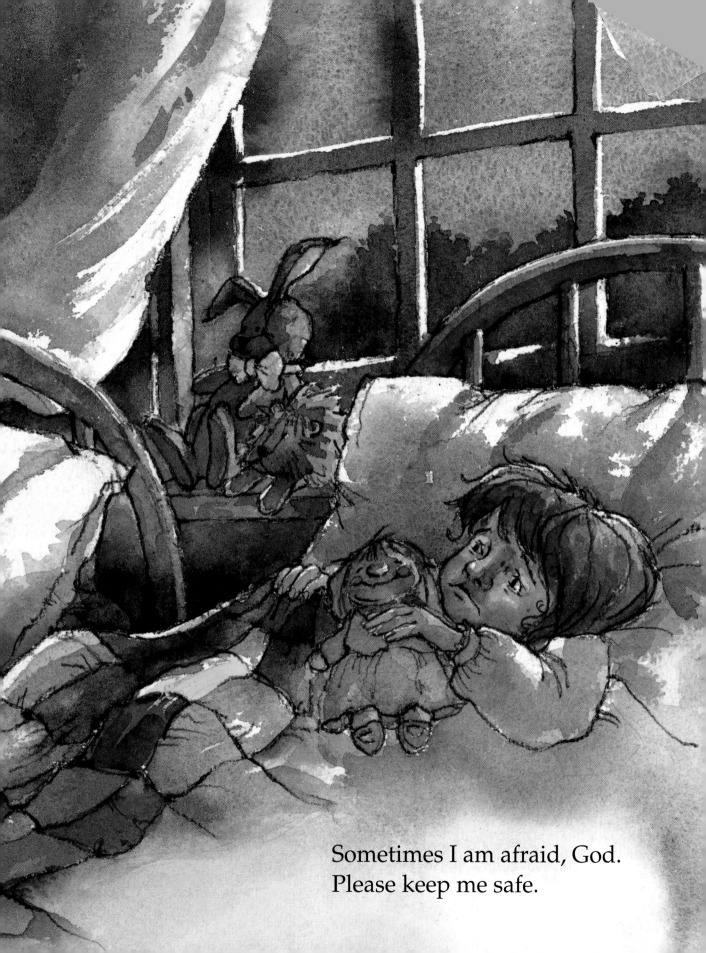

Sometimes I am afraid, God.
Please keep me safe.

For the kingdom, the power, and the glory are yours, now and forever. Amen

Everything in the world belongs to you, God!
You can do anything
and for that I thank you and say,
"Hooray!"

The Lord's Prayer with Selected Signs

Our **Father**, who art in **heaven**,

hallowed be thy **name**,

thy **kingdom** come,

thy **will** be done,

on **earth** as it is in **heaven**.

Give us this day our daily **bread**;

and **forgive** us our trespasses,

as we **forgive** those
who trespass against us;

and **lead** us not into temptation,
but deliver us from evil.

For thine is the **kingdom**,

and the **power**, and the **glory**,

forever and ever. **Amen**

When I Pray

Marie Ingham

Marie Ingham

When I pray soft and low, when I pray this I know,

God will al - ways hear, God will al - ways hear.

God Hears My Prayers

I know that God always hears my prayers.
My five fingers can remind me.

 God always is here.

 God always hears my prayers.

 God always understands me.

 God always forgives me.

 God always loves me.

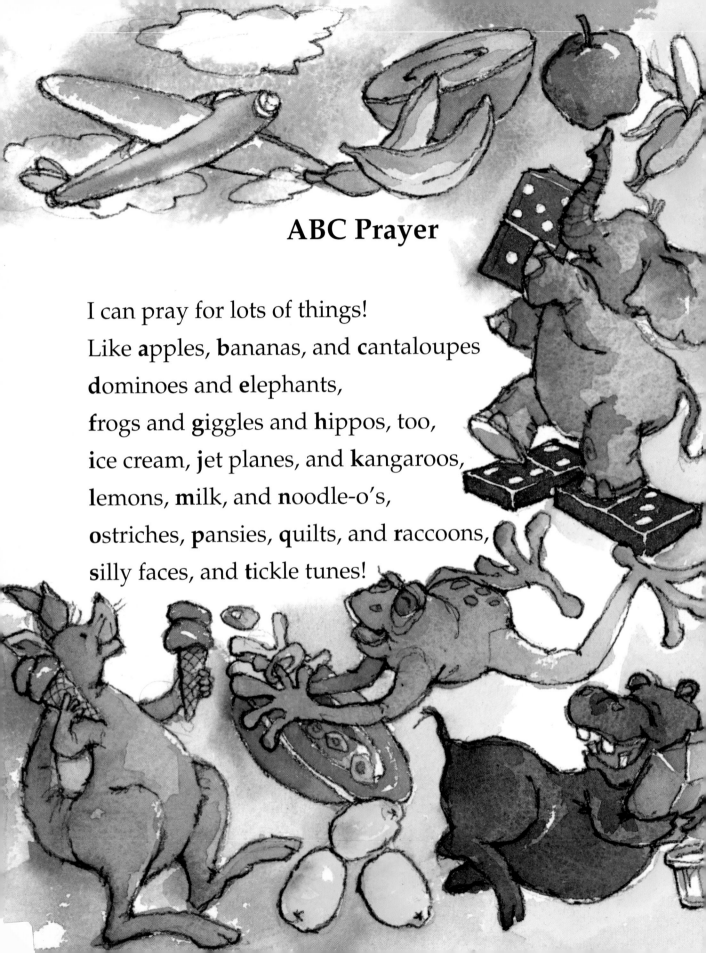

ABC Prayer

I can pray for lots of things!
Like **a**pples, **b**ananas, and **c**antaloupes
dominoes and **e**lephants,
frogs and **g**iggles and **h**ippos, too,
ice cream, **j**et planes, and **k**angaroos,
lemons, **m**ilk, and **n**oodle-o's,
ostriches, **p**ansies, **q**uilts, and **r**accoons,
silly faces, and **t**ickle tunes!

For **u**kuleles, **v**iolins,
walruses with double chins,
x-rays, **y**o-yo's on their strings,
and **z**ippers to zip coats and things!
Throughout the day and nighttime, too,
I can pray, and so can you!

Jesus Loves Me

Anna B. Warner (v. 1)
Debbie Trafton O'Neal (v. 2)

William S. Bradbury

1. Je - sus loves me, this I know, _ for the Bi - ble tells me so;
2. Je - sus taught us how to pray, to God our Fa - ther ev - ery day;

Lit - tle ones to him be - long, they are weak but he is strong.
Morn- ing, noon, and night-time, too, we can pray and so can you.

Yes, Je - sus loves me! Yes, Je - sus loves me!
Yes, we can pra - ay! Yes, we can pra - ay!

Yes, Je - sus loves me: the Bi - ble tells me so.
Yes, we can pra - ay: to God through-out the day.